That's Comical

'We were delighted to have the opportunity to work with Scoil Chaitríona 4th year students at the National Gallery of Ireland. Over several months the students became immersed in the Gallery's history, its ambiance and its collection. Inspired by their experience, they then created the stories contained in this wonderful book.'

Seán Love
Fighting Words

'The National Gallery of Ireland houses the national collection of Irish and European fine art. We were pleased to be a venue for a Fighting Words project with 21 Transition Year students from Scoil Chaitríona in 2013. Our staff were delighted to meet the students, bring them behind the scenes to see areas such as prints and drawings, conservation and the Centre for the Study of Irish Art, show them works of art from our collections and to see them interact with our creative practitioner. Their stories reflect their own distinctive creativity, energy and imaginations. We hope they continue to be creative and innovative and we wish them every success in the future.'

Sean Rainbird
Director of the National Gallery of Ireland

THAT'S COMICAL

An anthology of graphic fiction by students from Scoil Chaitríona, Glasnevin.

FIGHTING WORDS
THE WRITE TO RIGHT

A *Fighting Words* publication.

That's Comical is published in April 2014.

© Individual authors, 2014.

Fighting Words
Behan Square
Russell Street
Dublin 1
www.fightingwords.ie

Printed by: Hudson Killeen
Blanchardstown, Dublin 15

Interior and cover design:
Rosa Devine

No part of this book may be used or reproduced in any manner without written permission from the publisher, except in the context of reviews.

ISBN: 978-0-9568326-6-5

The National Gallery of Ireland wish to thank the *Matheson Giving Programme* for their support of Children's and Family Programmes at the National Gallery of Ireland.

Fighting Words gratefully acknowledges funding support from:

TABLE OF CONTENTS

Foreword by Rosa Devine ...viii

THE OFFICE CLERK ...1
Daire Bourke Boyle

THE ANTIVILLAIN ...11
David Cummins

SO CLOSE ...17
Pádraig Mac Eoin

THE ISLAND ...23
Jamie McCarthy

THE BUS JOURNEY ...31
Darragh Mc Laughlin

THE ENTERTAINER ...41
Moll McLaughlin

THE VOYAGE ...49
Jade Ní Bhroin

THE COUNTRY BOY ...57
Aoife Ní Chathmhaoil

THE MOVE ...63
Annagh Ní Cheallaigh

THE REBOUND ...67
Meadhbh Ní Dhálaigh

SAMMY'S DIARY ...73
Laoise Ní Dhonnchú

THE SIMPLE LIFE Holly Ní Fhianna	...81
A LESSON LEARNED Emily Ní Loinsigh	...89
THE PASS OF LIFE Stephanie Ní Shuailaí	...97
THE LAST DANCE Taminine Ní Mheachair	...105
FREEDOM Aoife Nic Chormaic	...113
LETTERS Aoife Nic Con Iomaire	...119
THE LAST ONE Sorcha Nic Giolla Rua	...127
EXCEPTION Cian Ó Donnabháin	...133
WAITING Ornaith O'Reilly	...139
THE DANCER IN THE PAINTING Colleen Whelan Fletcher	...149
Picture Gallery: The work in progress	...154

FOREWORD
By Rosa Devine

On Tuesday, 24th September 2013, a group of students from Scoil Chaitríona, Glasnevin, arrived in the National Gallery of Ireland to take part in an optional transition year project – to create their own comic book. Many of the students did not take art as a subject in school and few had ever read a comic book. Yet, they came together to create and to tell their own stories... every Tuesday, for nine weeks!

Their time in the gallery each week was split into two parts. During the first part they were treated to a tour of some aspect of the museum. Alongside carefully curated tours of current exhibitions they had the opportunity to visit and observe many behind-the-scenes aspects of the life of the gallery. Open and welcoming staff encouraged them to ask questions, look behind doors and to generally make the gallery a place of their own. And indeed they did. Whether in stories about art heists, about the nostalgia of a painter's model, or even about the art gallery as a place where a stressed-out teenager might go to reflect, the students of Scoil Chaitríona took ownership of their experiences in the gallery, often in quietly understated ways. To create art of their own was perhaps the most authentic possible response to their weekly exposure to the wonders of the National Gallery of Ireland.

The second half of their weekly afternoon in the gallery was devoted to artwork of their own creation. A team of dedicated volunteers from Fighting Words – joined by an education staff member, intern and enthusiastic creative practitioner from the gallery – were on hand to provide a sounding board for ideas, to assist working out technical issues and to provide encouragement when spirits flagged. More often than not, our job was simply to sit back in awe as a room full of young creatives blazed through the work of making their comic debut.

You hold in your hands an incredibly important moment - the first pressing of talent, raw and rich, distilled in a wonderfully imperfect, fly-by-instinct, tell-the-story-as-it-wants-to-be-told anthology of new comic work from new comic creators. This already great achievement is made all the more impressive by the fact that few, if any, of the creators of this book had more than a passing acquaintance with comics at the outset. Yet there is no sense of anxiety in the work that the authors have not spent years mastering the grammar of comics or slaving away at the craft of life drawing. Instead, they pared back the process – the limited time available would have would have been a tall order for even established cartoonists – and went straight for the heart of the creative arts, be it dance, poetry, sculpture or comics: storytelling.

And what stories! The variety of stories in this anthology is matched only by the variety of artistic execution. Daire Burke Boyle's story 'The Office Clerk', through confident drawing and minimal use of text, tells of one man's decision to quit his desk job and become a professional thief. He starts out small, nicking his villain costume in broad daylight, and quickly moves on to lifting some of the greatest treasures in the National Gallery of Ireland. The newly established thief makes a brief cameo in the next tale, 'The Antivillain' by David Cummins, before quickly coming to a sticky end. A similar fate awaits most unwanted characters at the hands of the spooky, malicious silhouette which haunts Cummins' dark and restrained artwork. Talent, insecurity, loss and escapism are central to Pádraig Mac Eoin's comic 'So Close', recounting the rise and fall of a young footballer with great potential who loses his father first and his sense of direction shortly after.

Silent, panoramic panels wonderfully rendered in coloured pencils give a sense of the cinematic to Jamie McCarthy's story about survival against the odds in 'The Island'. A chance meeting is the inspiration for 'The Bus Journey' by Darragh Mc Laughlin. It's a story that requires careful attention: many surprisingly small details carry story elements, perfectly contrasted with large and beautiful interpretations of the shared daydreams of strangers. 'The Entertainer' could be a daydream or make-believe adventure or maybe it really is 'reality' as perceived by a small child. Moll McLaughlin brilliantly exploits colour, style and layout to represent the sense of childhood and a child's world view.

Jade Ní Bhroin's 'The Voyage' is as much about the journey of growing up as the journey between countries. The simple and bright style of the artwork counterbalances some of the harsh realities of life depicted in the story. I am particularly fond of her use of the text as a visual component of the page. A young boy runs away to the big city for some perspective in Aoife Ní Chathmhaoil's 'The Country Boy'. The story is told through a mix of illustration, text and incredibly skilful collage and reminds us that distance is the perfect lens through which to identify that which is truly important to us. That few changes are as bad as we fear they will be is the moral of Annagh Ní Cheallaigh's comic 'The Move', subtly reinforced by her smart use of black and white artwork for the past and the protagonist's resistance to the move and colour artwork for the happier present.

Change and loss is also central to Meadhbh Ní Dhálaigh's story 'The Rebound' which makes no attempt to soften the fact that fate is often unkind to our dreams. An inspired use of silhouettes draws the reader into the energy and physicality of basketball and, at the moment of impact, the silhouettes immediately give way to fuller drawings better suited to deal with the vulnerability of the human form. A mixture of collage and drawing, with lovely soft pencil work, sets the mood for 'Sammy's Diary' by Laoise Ní Dhonnchú, exploring our universal need for security. It would be hard to imagine a more perfect closing image for this story than the strong, graphic portrayal of the meaning of family on the final page. Holly Ní Fhianna's story 'The Simple Life' is a hilarious tale of the stubbornness of teenagers and you cannot help but relate to her brilliant portrayal of the frustrated father. The restrained use of only lead pencil to tell this entertaining story creates a sense of lightness on the page that is well suited to the whimsy of the content. Never lie about ghosts is the lesson in Emily Ní Loinsigh's 'A Lesson Learned'. Fabulous colour, layout and lettering creates a really appealing and distinctive style for this comic about a prank between new friends.

'The Pass of Life' by Stephanie Ní Shuailaí is a charming tale about how a minor obstacle such as your own death need not come between you and achieving your dreams of true love, romance and a glittering career. Taminine Ní Mheachair's 'The Last Dance' is a tour de force of stunning colour work which really pulls you into a few short moments of story which are both eerie and bittersweet. The struggle for autonomy as an adolescent, something every reader can relate to, is the inspiration for 'Freedom' by Aoife Nic Chormaic. It was tempting to send a photocopy of 'Freedom' to every TD: when teenagers are so often viewed with suspicion in public places, this story shows the importance of public space as a place for young people to reflect on their relationship with themselves and those around them.

Aoife Nic Con Iomaire's highly stylised comic 'Letters', about a prison warden who decides to come between an inmate and his attractive wife, combines confident use of her chosen medium with an intriguing premise about the abuse of trust and power. Dark and witty, 'The Last One' is an absurdist comic by Sorcha Nic Giolla Rua which will be worryingly understandable to many tea drinkers. Her use of the central topic, tea, as the medium with which she adds colour to her pages is nothing short of inspired. A robot dystopia is the setting for 'Exception', a future imagining of our world where an impenetrable wall of programmed 'trashcans' stands between the average citizen and the ruling elite. The strength of Cian Ó Donnabháin's concept is such that, in a few short pages, he easily conveys a world, a history and a very unsettling future.

Portrayed by an effective combination of photographic people and illustrative cats and clockwork, 'Waiting' by Ornaith O'Reilly is a reminder of the importance of punctuality through the vivid depiction of the anxiety of waiting for someone who is late returning home. Finally, 'The Dancer in the Painting' presents an oft-overlooked perspective on art - that of the painter's model. Colleen Whelan Fletcher tells a warming story of a retired model who, on finding a painting of herself hanging in an art gallery, is transported backwards to a time in her life when her passion for dance was all-consuming and anything seemed possible.

Fighting Words, a centre for creative writing where thousands of stories begin their lives each year; the National Gallery of Ireland, where centuries of visual art is displayed for generations of people. A group of impressively talented young people blended the essence of these two organisations and produced something which is not 'of' high art, great literature, their school, their tutors, Fighting Words or the National Gallery of Ireland but entirely of their own creative voice. I recommend you hold this book with both hands.

DAIRE BOURKE BOYLE

Daire Bourke Boyle is 16 years old. He loves good music and enjoys drawing and art in general. One of his great dislikes is pointless music. Cook him a good meal and you'll probably win him over. Also, he has a phenomonal phobia of people pulling cotton wool apart.

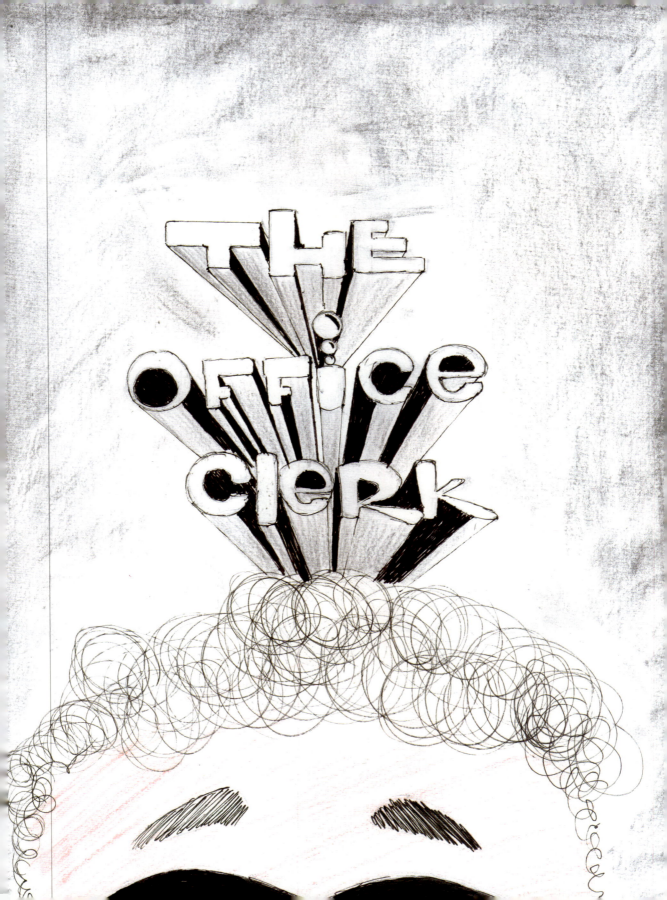

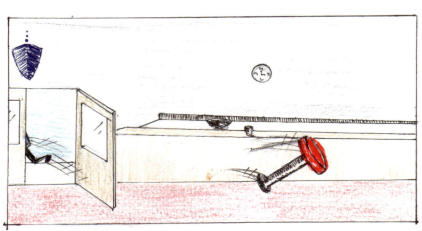

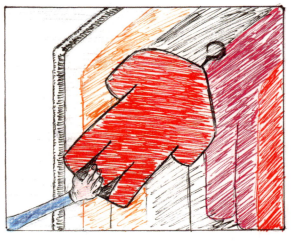

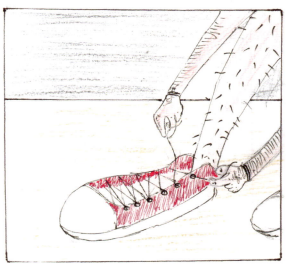
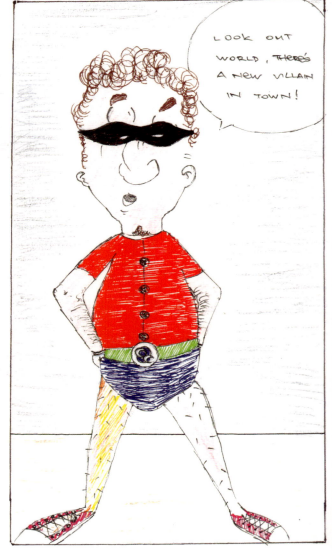
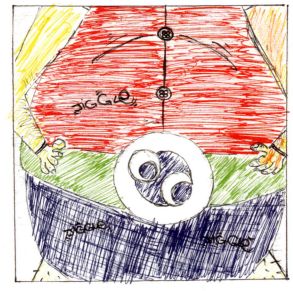

DAVID CUMMINS

My name is David, I'm from Glasnevin North. I enjoy long walks on the beach and I'm waiting for that special someone… I listen to loads of different types of music except for house and dubstep. It's not music, it's just noise.

THE ANTIVILLAIN

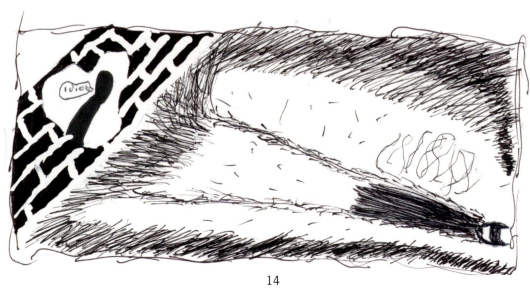

PADRAIG MAC EOIN

Padraig Mac Eoin is 16, from Marino. He lives with his parents and his sister. He plays GAA for St Vincent's. He always puts the milk into the bowl before the cereal. If he had to pick he would say that the best ninja turtle was Raphael.

The change was amazing, I was worlds apart from where I was when I started, I felt invincible.

That was until............!!

JAMIE MCCARTHY

My name is Jamie McCarthy and I am 15 years old. I am also a superhero. My favourite food is pancakes and I live on Mars. My sidekick is a talking donkey from Jupiter.

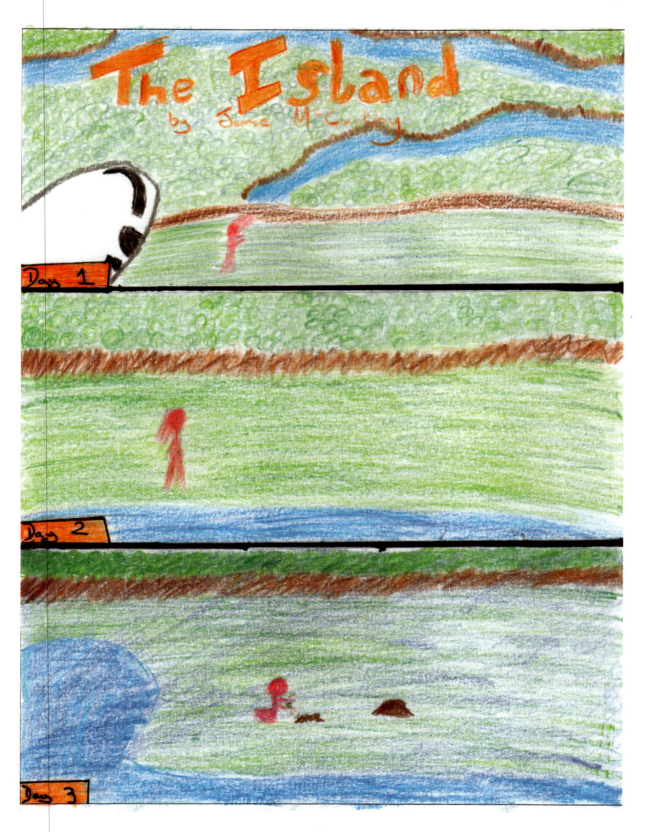

DARRAGH MC LAUGHLIN

Darragh Mc Laughlin is 16 years old and lives at home with his family. He likes to stay classy and dresses in the finest of suits. He is also partial to wining and dining the most beautiful of women. He also takes pride in his hair and embraces classiness.

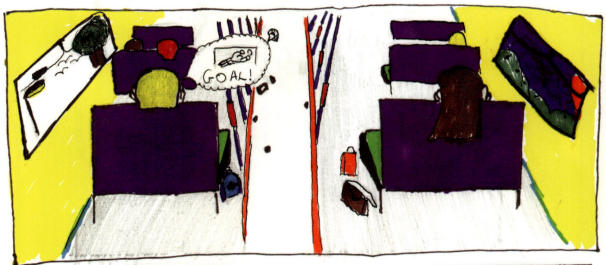

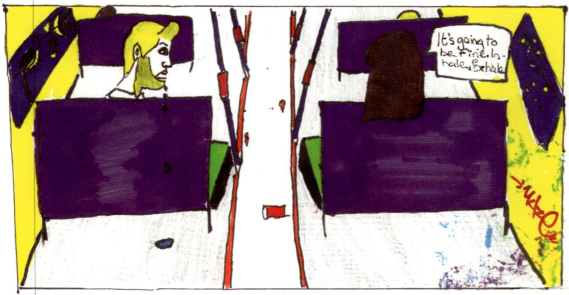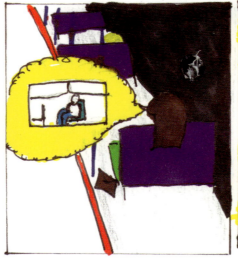

First home

Wedding Day

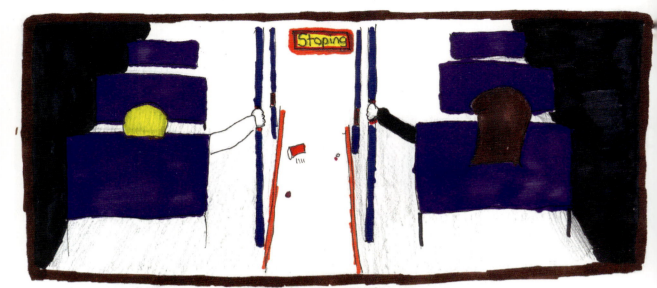

MOLL MCLAUGHLIN

Hi my name is Moll. I am 15 years old from Dublin. I love my fish Suzie, playing and listening to music and drinking hot Ribena.

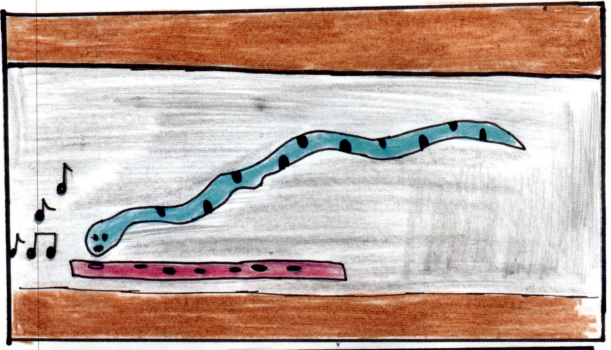

JADE NÍ BHROIN

I'm Jade and I'm 15. I have too many brothers and a sister. I have a phobia of ears and bad drawing skills. I play camogie and complain a lot. I got this story from my grandad so it's probably not true.

The Voyage.

So many of us and no food

No proper clothes

And no room in bed

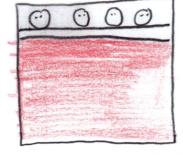

And the journey began

Dublin

NY

I decided to go sightseeing

When disaster struck

I was broke and alone. There was no choice.

The American dream was gone. I was homeward bound

The journey over...

There was still so many and no food

No proper clothes

And still no room in bed

But none of it mattered because I was home with my family

AOIFE NÍ CHATHMHAOIL

Hi, I'm Aoife, I'm 15 and I have big glasses. I go to Scoil Chaitríona, I'm in fourth year, with Llama and Awn. This journey was very stressful and a lot of work. Yes, I left everything to the last minute because I'm a typical teenage girl. I'm glad I took part! I love my best friends Sorcha and Annagh. Thank you for reading. Enjoy! :)

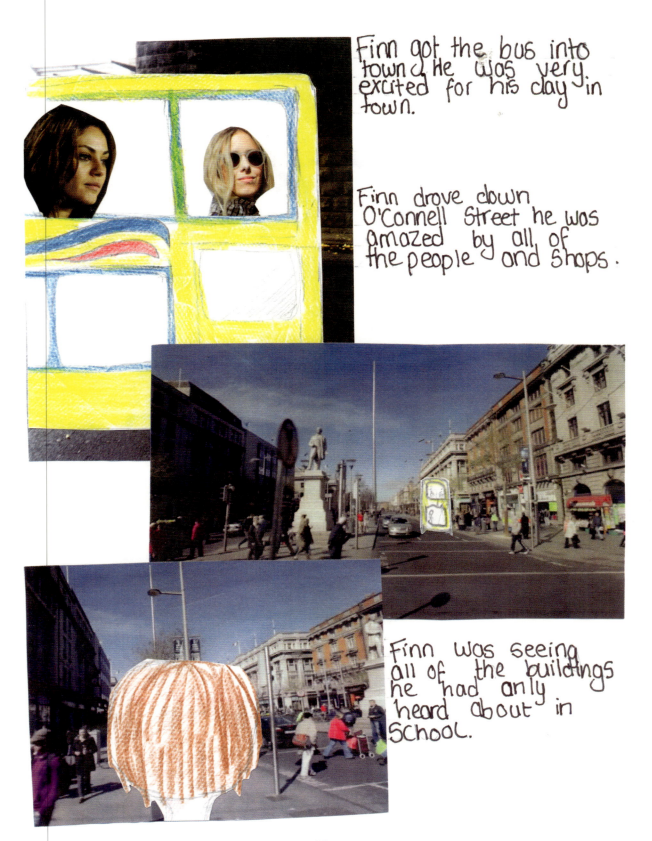

Finn got the bus into town. He was very excited for his day in town.

Finn drove down O'Connell Street he was amazed by all of the people and shops.

Finn was seeing all of the buildings he had only heard about in school.

Finn wandered around the city exploring the shops and roads.

He now understood what he was working for in school.

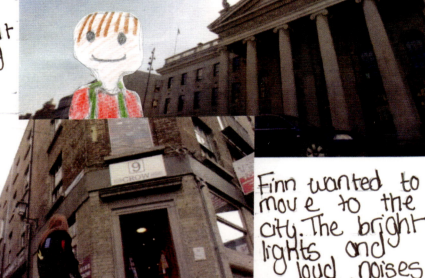

Finn wanted to move to the city. The bright lights and loud noises excited him.

Finn was walking by Croke Park, when he saw a dog. The dog ran over to Finn. The dog reminded Finn of his own dog Holly.

He now remembered the one thing he loved at home, his dog Holly.

He loved his day in the city but he wanted to go home and see Holly.

ANNAGH NÍ CHEALLAIGH

My name is Annagh and I am a 16 year old Galway girl living in Dublin! I love food especially chocolate, oh and I love tea! This experience has been reaaallly stressful but very interesting and enjoyable at the same time! Special shout out to my two amigos who always come to my house and eat my food! Love you gals! But I'm gunna go now because I dislike my handwriting. So byeee! Enjoy! x

THE MOVE

DUBLIN →

MEADHBH NÍ DHÁLAIGH

My name is Meadhbh Ní Dhálaigh. I am sixteen years old and am in fourth year in Scoil Chaitríona.

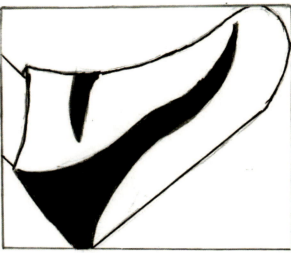

CRACK

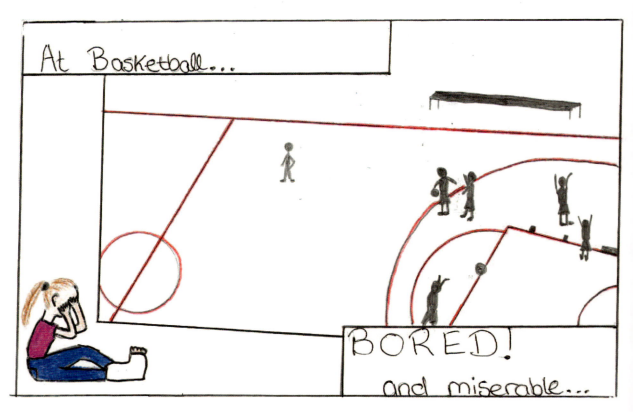

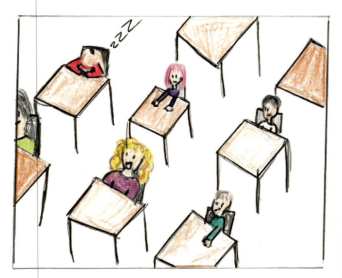

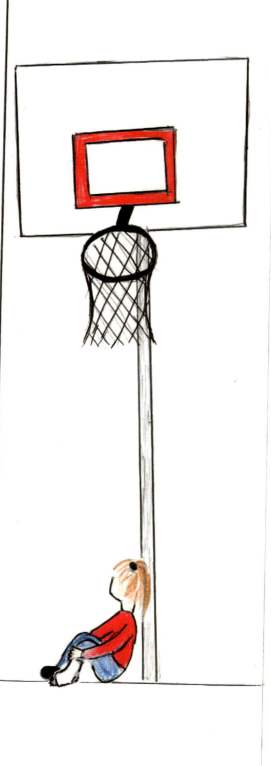

LAOISE NÍ DHONNCHÚ

My name's Laoise, I'm 15 years old and currently living in Dublin with my Mam, my Dad, my two sisters and my brother. I'm in Scoil Chaitríona in fourth year. I love playing camogie with my friends, listening to music and going to concerts. I enjoyed the experience of being part of this project and found it very interesting.

Dear Diary

Today Mam and Dad had a big fight! Rosie told me in school that once her Mam and Dad had a big fight and now they don't never talk and don't even live together anymore!!! What am I going to do without Mam and Dad?!? We do EVERYTHING together!! What if after they break up they don't want me anymore? What if they go and find new families and leave me all alone? I can't live without →<u>MY</u>← family!

Hopefully this concert I'm going to with Rosie and Kate will make me feel a little better!

I'll ask Rosie if her Mam and Dad found new families and left her by herself.

I'm too scared to ask Mam or Dad in case they get mad at me and have another fight!

I love them so much and I <u>hate</u> it when they fight!

lots of love
Sammy! ♡ xo

~~FIGHTING~~

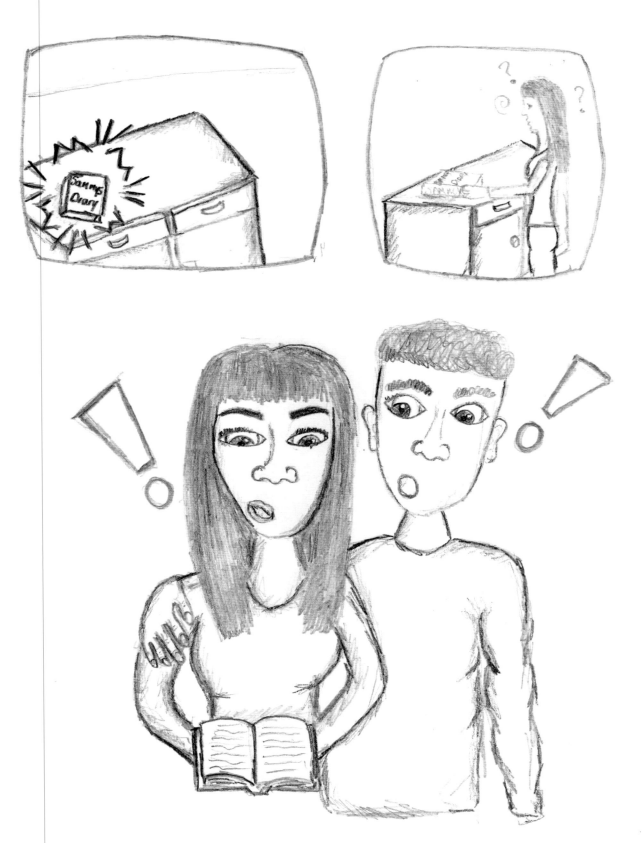

Dear Diary,
The concert last night was brilliant and Rosie told me that her Mam and Dad loved her just as much after they broke up even though they weren't together anymore.
While I was at the concert last night Mam found this diary. She sat me down with Dad and explained to me that no matter how many fights we all have we will ALWAYS be family and that if you really love someone you'll forgive them for their mistakes.
She told me that nearly everyone fights with the people they love, but the get over those fights because they love eachother. This reminded me of all the fights I'd ever had with my family and friends.
That's when I realised, family is forever.....
   love Sammy! ♡ xo

HOLLY NÍ FHIANNA

Holly Ní Fhianna is sixteen and lives in Dublin with her mam, dad & older brother. She enjoys Irish dancing, eating chocolate, half days on Wednesdays & singing (although some would rather she didn't).

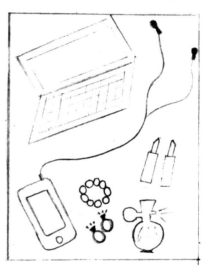

EMILY NÍ LOINSIGH

Emily Ní Loinsigh is 16 from Dublin. She lives with her mom, dad and twin sister. She enjoys chicken royale Tuesday, red cabbage and playing GAA. She hates when too many people speak at the same time.

A Lesson Learned

Tommy told them that a little scary dead girl was at the end of his bed when he woke up the night before. It worked, he had made friends!

The banging woke Tommy up suddenly. He was terrified.

Outside his window he saw a little ghostly girl, just like he told his friends he saw!

STEPHANIE NÍ SHUAILAÍ

I'm Stephanie Ní Shuailaí and I enjoy watching anime and reading manga. I love to watch action movies, gaming and hanging out with my friends and boyfriend.

ARIANA IS A POPULAR, HONOUR STUDENT. SHE HAS GREAT FRIENDS AND IS A GREAT ARTIST BUT ALL OF THAT WAS ABOUT TO CHANGE....

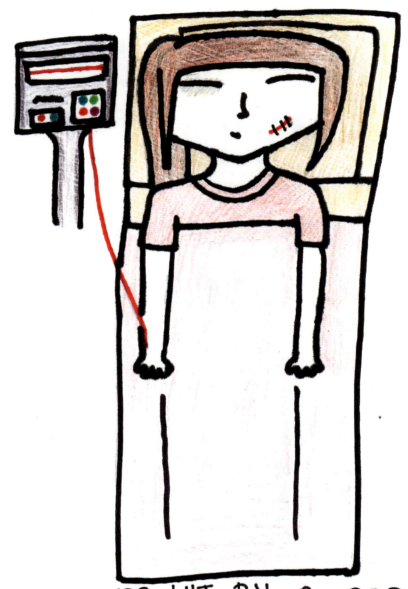

ARIANA WAS HIT BY A CAR ON HER WAY HOME FROM SCHOOL AND DIED TWO DAYS LATER.

SHE WAS ON HER WAY......

ARIANA COULDN'T BELIEVE HER EYES. IN FRONT OF HER STOOD HER GUARDIAN ANGEL. THIS WAS HER CHOICE, TO LEAVE WITH HIM TO HEAVEN OR RELIVE HER LIFE IN THE DEPT OF THE DEVIL.

ARIANA CHOSE TO FOLLOW HER GUARDIAN ANGEL TO HEAVEN AND STUDY TO BE A GUARDIEN ANGEL JUST lIKE HIM.

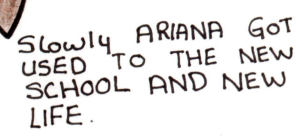

Slowly Ariana got used to the new school and new life.

Her new look and her wings needed more work to get used to but with her new friends and guardian, Alejandro, she slowly got used to it.

But Alejandro isin't just her guardian

ARIANA GRADUATED ANGEL ACADEMY AND BECAME A GUARDIAN ANGEE

ARIANA'S GUARDED CHILD LIVED A LIFE OF GREED AND DIS-HONEST HE BEGGED HER TO ALLOW HIM THE PASSAGE BACK TO HIS LIFE

ALEJANDRO EXPLANED TO HER THAT SHE CAN NOT ARGUE WITH HER GUARDED CHILD AND ALLOW HIM HIS CHOICE

SO ARIANA OPENED THE GATE TO HELL FOR HIM TO LET HIM MAKE HIS DEAL WITH THE DEVIL

Not all life can continue but just because you left, doesn't mean your done...

You can still make happy ever after happen.

TAMININE NÍ MHEACHAIR

I'm Taminine and I'm 15. I love music, books and really bad jokes. Did you hear about the girl with no friends? Apparently she's pun-bearable. Not unlike myself.

AOIFE NIC CHORMAIC

My name is Aoife, I'm 16 this year. My hobbies consist of going to concerts, taking pictures and fangirling. I like to be as optimistic as I can about everything.

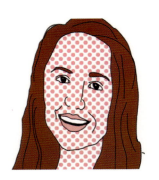

AOIFE NIC CON IOMAIRE

Hi! My name is Aoife Nic Con Iomaire. I am fifteen years old. I live in Druncondra with my Mam, Dad and my little sister. I play football and camogie for Na Fianna. I like going out to my friends and watching movies. This is my story and I hope you enjoy it. :)

Letters
By Aoife Nic Con Iomaire

Mrs. Crawley visits her husband for the first time in prison.

SORCHA NIC GIOLLA RUA

Sorcha Nic Giolla Rua is 16 years old. She lives with her parents and brother Ste. She is artistically challenged and loves tea. She plays the piano and enjoys going to Annagh's house after school with Aoife.

The Last One

I UNDERSTOOD WHY Ste KILLED ME.

I COULD SYMPATHISE.

CIAN Ó DONNABHÁIN

My name is Cian Ó Donnabháin. I am a 4th year student in Scoil Chaitríona. I am very interested in computers and technology and I based my graphic novel on these interests. I thoroughly enjoyed the Fighting Words course as it gave me a change to experience graphic storytelling, something I never had a chance to do before.

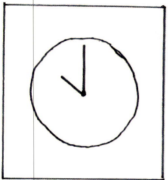

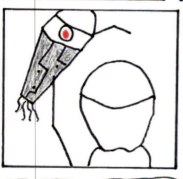

As more people lost their jobs, slums began to form.

The rich moved out of the city and created their own metropolis on top of a mountain, surrounded by a giant wall, the slums were out of sight and out of mind.

ORNAITH O'REILLY

Ornaith O'Reilly is a 15 year old girl. She lives with her Mam, Dad and three sisters. She loves tea, hates long walks with no destination and prefers J-Os to Oreos.

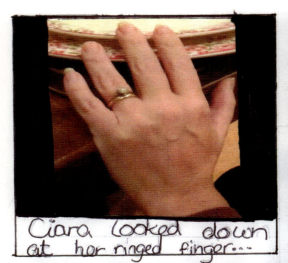 

Ciara looked down at her ringed finger... | and back at the immaculate kitchen

The table was extravagantly set | The smell of beef casserole filled the kitchen

 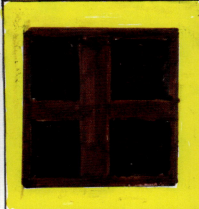 

Wine was waiting in the wine cooler | Outside a vicious storm raged | But the kitchen was bathed in candle light

Ciara however was slouched in her seat staring ahead

Her perfectly manicured fingers were fidgeting with the ends of her freshly blowdried hair. A recurring habit that arose when Ciara was nervous

She blinked back tears and took deep calming breaths

kitty slouched into the room from the open window

People commented on what a pity that the black tail ruined the innocent effect

Ciara however liked to think it represented her playful and rebelious nature

Kitty was free unlike Ciara who felt trapped waiting for her husband every Friday night.

Kitty's stare made Ciara feel two feet tall. Ashamed. Ciara knew that she should confront her husband about coming home late

Her heart filled with determination as she rose to greet him and she knew that she would never allow him to come home late without telling her again

COLLEEN WHELAN FLETCHER

My name is Colleen Whelan Fletcher, I'm 16 years old and live in Finglas. I play the guitar and I have trained in ballet for over ten years. I also love movies and animals.

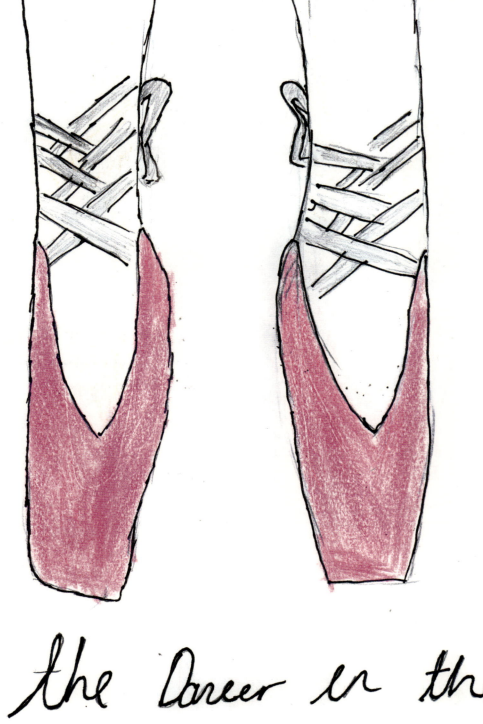

the Dancer in the Painting.

PICTURE GALLERY
The work in progress

ACKNOWLEDGEMENTS

Thank you to all the team from Fighting Words; Nicola Colton, Rosa Devine, Jean Hanney, Orla Lehane, Aine Mannion, Duffy Mooney Sheppard, Adrienne Quinn, and Alan Worrall.

Thank you to Caoilte O Mahony, Niamh Donellan, Andrew Brown, Joanne Drum, Caomhán Mac Con Iomaire and all the members of the National Gallery of Ireland staff who met with and guided us on tours of the gallery. Further thanks to the Director of the National Gallery of Ireland, Mr.Sean Rainbird, and to Dr. Marie Bourke, Keeper and Head of Education.

Thank you to our principal, Caitríona Ní Laighean, vice principal, Carmel de Grae, TY Coordinator, Charlie Diver, and all the staff of the school. We are especially grateful to our teacher Patricia Wall.

ADDITIONAL IMAGE CREDITS

Pages 7 and 8:
Michelangelo Merisi da Caravaggio (1571-1610)
The Taking of Christ, 1602, courtesy of the National
Gallery of Ireland and the Jesuit Community of
Leeson Street, Dublin, who acknowledge the
generosity of the late Dr Marie Lea-Wilson.
Photo © National Gallery of Ireland.

Page 154:
John Butler Yeats (1839-1922), *Pippa Passes,*
(illustration for Browning's poem of 1841), 1869-71.
Photo © National Gallery of Ireland.

Page 155:
Edgar Degas (1834-1917), *Two Ballet Dancers in a
Dressing Room,* c.1880.
Photo © National Gallery of Ireland.

Page 156:
William Orpen (1878-1931), *Lady with a
Birdcage,* 1903.
Photo © National Gallery of Ireland.

Page 157:
James Malton (1761-1803), *St. Patrick's Cathedral,
Dublin, South-East View from the Churchyard,* 1793.
Photo © National Gallery of Ireland.

Frederic Burton (1816-1900), *A Bavarian Peasant
Girl,* 1850s.
Photo © National Gallery of Ireland.

Strickland Lowry (1737-c.1785), *The Spartan Boy
(Trompe L'Oeil),* after 1775.
Photo © National Gallery of Ireland.

Page 158:
National Gallery of Ireland Millennium Wing (2002).
Photo © National Gallery of Ireland.